The Arfabet!

A book of dog poems from A to Z

By TJ Farrell

Illustrated by Aram Joao
and Almir Ulises Mestre León

The Arfabet!
A book of dog poems from A to Z

Copyright © 2024 TJ Farrell

All rights reserved. No part of this publication may be reproduced, stored in a retrieval system, or transmitted, in any form or by any means, electronic, mechanical, photo-copying, recording, or otherwise, without the written prior permission of the author.

All images, logos, quotes, and trademarks included in this book are subject to use according to trademark and copyright laws of the United States of America.

Illustrations by Aram Joao and Almir Ulises Mestre León

Interior Design and Layout by Pamela McKinnie, Concepts Unlimited

ISBN: 979-8-218-46362-5 (pbk)

All rights reserved by TJ FARRELL
and Half Moon Cat Publishing
This book is printed in the United States of America

Dedication

This book is dedicated to Bruce Allen: poet, teacher, lifelong friend, and the first grown-up who ever said to me, "You know, you don't have to do all the hard stuff at once, you could lighten up on yourself a bit." Without you, Bruce, this book would only have lived in my computer, with bits occasionally trotted out for literary events at coffee shops. Thank you for cheering it on, saying that you wanted to see it in print, finding a publisher for it, and all the decades of unwavering belief and kind words.

Do you know the Arfabet?

You've heard about the Alphabet
The letters A to Z,
I hope that you won't be upset
If I take liberties,
By matching up the letters
Of the alphabet to dogs
Like Papillons and Setters
When I'm done with this prologue

For this is the "Arfabet"
And every poem in here,
Names a buddy or a pet
That somebody holds dear

Fuzzy, shaggy, bald, or curly
There are some of every type,
Dogs that work and get up early,
Pups of every hue and stripe

The poems are all kinds of verse
From triolets to haiku
Some are "doggerel" or worse
I hope that this won't bug you!
So let's explore some dogs with rhyme
And maybe share a smile,
We'll have ourselves a lovely time
In Arfabet-y style!

A is for Afghan Hound

The Afghan is regal and wears his hair long,

He runs like the wind on legs swift and strong

He carries himself with canine nobility

Like a king in his cape of responsibility

His stately good looks cannot be denied,

Afghans are aloof but quite dignified

A is for Alaskan Malamute

The dog of the North! Through the snow and the fog,

A Malamute's job is a freight-pulling dog

With a thick double coat of cozy warm fur,

A snowy cold day is what he prefers

He's loyal and steadfast and loves to have fun,

And the Malamute's strength is second to none

B is for Basenji

With a furrowed brow, and a curled tail,

A Basenji won't bark; he'll yodel and wail

He's curious and clever; some might say a brat,

And can jump to the countertop, just like a cat

If a Basenji wants something up in a tree

He may climb up after it, one-two-three!

B is for Border Collie

A Border Collie's a reliable canine,

He works hard with his shepherd all day and won't whine

As working dogs, Border Collies are diligent,

They're fast and they're strong and very intelligent

If you want a dog that works hard for his keep

And need an assistant to help herd your sheep

A Border Collie's just the dog that can work it

Or he'll place first on the agility circuit

Desire to please, and intense concentration,

Make them winning athletes of great reputation

C is for Chinese Crested

The Chinese Crested may cause some anxieties,

For he comes in two very surprising varieties!

The Powderpuff has hair all over his form,

But the Hairless one needs a wool coat to stay warm

With only a crest and a tail plume and socks

Made of feathery fur in long silky locks,

The Hairless variety must be concerned,

For without some sunscreen, he will get sunburned!

C is for Collie

(A triolet poem)

You have to love the gentle Collie,

So smart, alert, and reliable

Good at herding, and usually jolly,

You have to love the gentle Collie

They guard their family so carefully,

And their beauty's undeniable

You have to love the gentle Collie,

So smart, alert, and reliable

D is for Dachshund

A Dachshund is a "badger dog"

Who hails from Germany

He can be a stubborn pup

Though he loves his family

Your basic Doxie's long and low

But fast and rarely shy

There is a stout courageous heart

Inside that little guy!

He was bred for hunting badgers

And other game for sport

And doesn't think there's anything

Wrong with being short

Whether he is out for work or play

He's set in his mentality

You're sure to smile a lot because

He's full of personality!

D is for Dalmatian

To run for miles beside a coach

Is what a Dalmatian's born to do

His loyalty and bold approach

Make him a first-rate watchdog, too

He's strong and active; it's no surprise,

A Dalmatian will run through rain and muck

By his spots, you'll recognize

The dog that rides the fire truck!

E is for English Cocker Spaniel

The English Cocker jaunts around

In the country or the town

He's merry and active, though small in size,

With a silky coat and soft brown eyes

If you would roam the countryside,

To find where pheasants like to hide,

And have a dog to seek them, then you'll

Need an English Cocker Spaniel!

E is for English Setter

The English Setter is versatile

He's a gentle and devoted friend

Long and graceful and full of style,

A dog on which you can depend

With his freckly face and his feathery tail

In the field or at home or at play,

The English Setter stands by without fail

Your staunch joyful friend every day!

F is for Finnish Spitz

A frisky dog of golden red

With a face that looks like a fox,

The Finnish Spitz roves far ahead

When hunting, and Oh! How he talks!

Quietly first, he woofs very low,

Then louder, as loud as he can!

Where the ice and the snow

And the cold winds will blow

He's the national dog of Finland

F is for French Bulldog

Do you like a dog with ears like a bat,

And a head that is solid and square?

If so, a French Bulldog's what you'd like to pat,

He's muscular with short, clean, smooth hair

Although he looks a bit like a gargoyle,

He's friendly and makes a good pet,

A Frenchie's an excellent watchdog and loyal,

With a face you could never forget!

G is for German Shepherd

German Shepherds are the K-9 select,

To search and to serve and protect

They work with policemen

To hunt down the villains

And sniff out what we can't detect

The Shepherd's good manners always dictate

Their behavior must be first-rate

They're playful and smart,

With loving big hearts,

As family dogs, Shepherds are great!

G is for Great Dane

The Great Dane is a gentle giant,

He was bred to hunt wild boars

Sweet and dignified and self-reliant

He's at home both in and outdoors

Many say among dogs he is king,

So elegant, calm, and well-bred,

The Dane's a great friend, but here's the thing,

You'll need lots of food when he's fed!

H is for Harrier

The Harrier chases rabbits and hares,

That's how he got his name,

He runs with his pack in the fresh morning air,

And his skill at the hunt is his fame

He's a hardworking hound who needs exercise

As a sprinter, he won't be outdone,

So if you have found he's your dog, I'd advise

You plan to take him for a run!

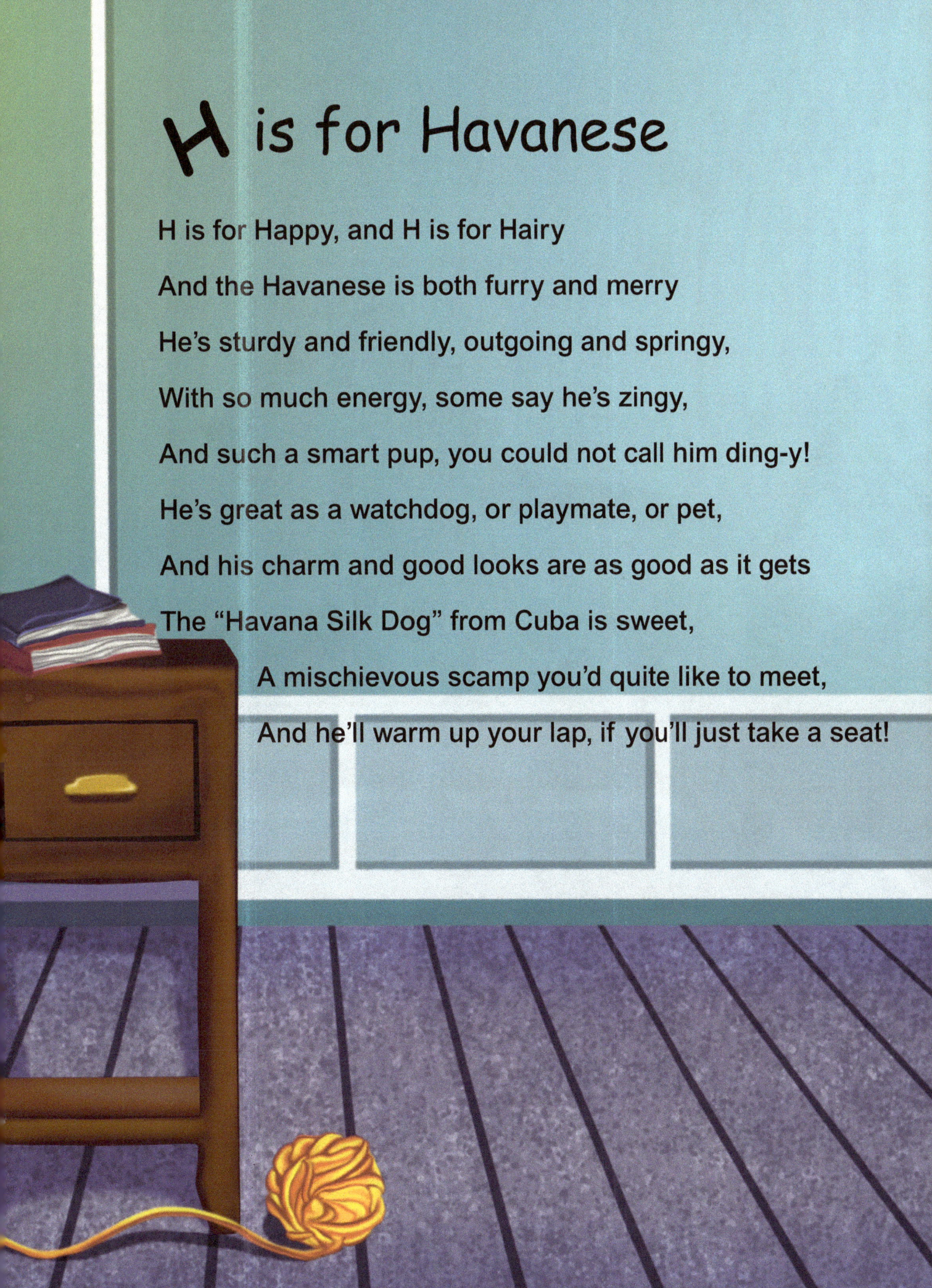

H is for Havanese

H is for Happy, and H is for Hairy

And the Havanese is both furry and merry

He's sturdy and friendly, outgoing and springy,

With so much energy, some say he's zingy,

And such a smart pup, you could not call him ding-y!

He's great as a watchdog, or playmate, or pet,

And his charm and good looks are as good as it gets

The "Havana Silk Dog" from Cuba is sweet,

A mischievous scamp you'd quite like to meet,

And he'll warm up your lap, if you'll just take a seat!

I is for Irish Wolfhound

The peaceful giants of Ireland,

Irish Wolfhounds are ever so grand

With a wide chest in front,

They are keen for a hunt,

And always appear in command

If you walk with a Wolfhound it's rare,

For other people not to stare,

Because they have found

That from ears to the ground,

Your hound is the tallest dog there!

I is for Italian Greyhound

Would you like a little dog that is sporty and sleek?

Who looks just like a racing dog, but tiny?

A peppy puppy popping with a pretty impish streak,

Who can jump up high enough to pat your heinie?

I can tell you'd really love the chic Italian Greyhound,

To carry and to cuddle all the time,

She's ziggy and she's zaggy and her tail is really waggy

And she twirls like a tornado on a dime!

J is for Japanese Chin
(Sort of a Haiku)

The Japanese Chin

Dog of aristocracy

Lively, stylish, soft

Smiling mouth,

Loves to sit in laps

Comforting

Playful companion

And Imperial Court pet

Chin are royalty

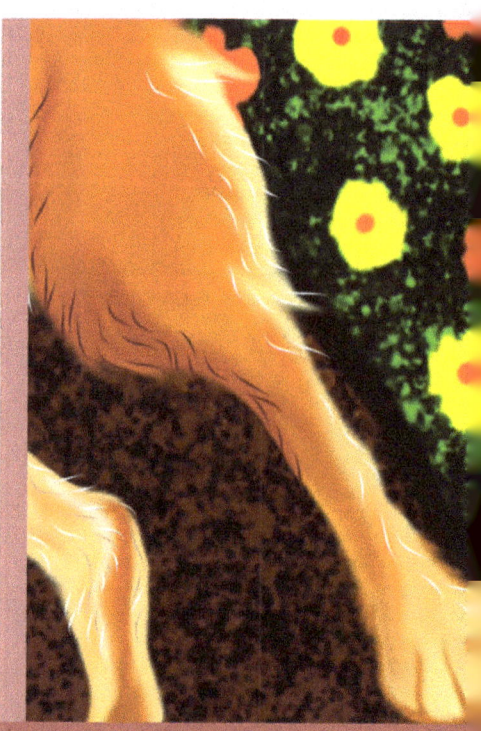

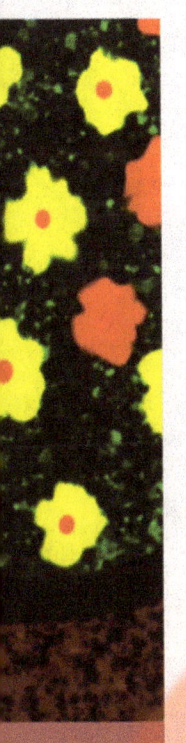

J is for Jindo

There's a Jindo

At my window

Should I let him

Come on in, though?

He's a hunter come to see ya

From an island off Korea,

And back home he's earned his measure,

He is hailed a national treasure

He's a handful to contain, though,

Be prepared to love and train, so

Read about him if you don't know

A lot about the noble Jindo

K is for Keeshond

Richly maned like furry lions,

Keeshonds strut their ruffs with pride

They march along, cream, black, and gray

With their brisk, assertive stride

Handsome with their gray-ringed eyes,

Marching through the throng,

What a grand parade it is,

As the Keeshonds go rolling along!

K is for Kuvasz

Polite and noble and somewhat reserved

The Kuvasz is ready to guard or to herd

They're never found to be lacking in nerve

These gorgeous white dogs are longing to serve

They hail from Hungary, and also Tibet,

Their name is from Turkey; how international can you get?

Kuvaszok are suspicious of those they've not met,

But this loving big dog makes a very good pet

L is for Labrador Retriever

She's your buddy, she's your pal

She's your Lab and loves to play

Fetch the stick! Go get it gal!

She'll bring back that stick all day!

Black or Yellow, Chocolate too

Labradors are always there

They can run fast and pursue

You will always be a pair!

Through the woods and in the lake

Your Lab Retriever loves it all,

And in just minutes she will make

A soggy doggy tennis ball!

L is for Löwchen

Who's that little dog with the hairy lion's mane?

He's so bright and lively but how do you say his name?

It kind of sounds like "lotion," with a German emphasis

And it means "little lion," but I would be remiss

If I didn't tell you how inquisitive he is!

The Löwchen is a lapdog, and good for warming feet

You can style their front just like a mane with short hair on their seat,

Though they like a lot of brushing to keep them tangle free,

In between they like to play and keep you company,

And they can charm most anyone, wouldn't you agree?

M is for Mastiff

A Mastiff is a massive dog

For guarding hearth and home

He's found in ancient histories of

England, Egypt and Rome

Strong and gentle; loyal to

His friends and family

Be sure you give him room to sprawl

He'll do so happily

Walk him 'round your neighborhood

And I can guarantee

He'll impress the folks you meet

With quiet dignity

M is for Mutt

The Mutt! The Mutt! Everyone's Dog!

A mix of whatever you like,

Small as a teapot or round as a log

Named Maddy or Scruffy or Spike!

In baskets, in farmyards, in parks, and on boats

Working or playing a game,

So many sizes and colors and coats

And never two looking the same

You gotta love Mutts, they're smart and they're fun

A hodgepodge of doggie genetics

Each one is a new thing under the sun

To broaden your canine aesthetics!

N is for Newfoundland
(A name poem)

Newfies love water

Everyone oughter

Watch how they swim in a pool

Fun-loving playmate

Or hardworking heavyweight

Unparalleled monarch of drool

Newfies have sweet

Dispositions and meet

Loved ones with a big smile

Always very smart

Naturally big hearts

Dogs that are quite versatile!

N is for Norwich Terrier

A wee bonny lass is the terrier from Norwich,

She hails from England, and her name sounds like "porridge"

A gutsy hunt terrier

Or a pup in a carrier

She's fearless at work or at play

Don't be fooled by the size of this Lady

She's certainly never a 'fraidy!

She's charming and loyal,

And struts like she's royal,

She's your partner in crime every day!

O is for Old English Sheepdog

Shuffling through the square
This dog strolls without a care
But can he see at all behind that hair?
Well, he's used to peeking through it
And that is why he grew it
So he's better off if you just leave it there!

Now, he likes a weekly brushing
And as long as you're not rushing
You can spin it into yarn and make a sweater
It might be hard to maintain
And if you wore it in the rain
Would you smell just like a doggie in wet weather?

O is for Otterhound

The Otterhound is a loveable klutz
He's shaggy but shouldn't be grouped with the mutts
He has webbed feet and a deep-voiced bay
And a nose so discerning
It can be concerning
For it really could lead him astray!

Now don't be surprised
If he seems quite disguised
By his beard full of mud, twigs, and moss
Just remember to say,
"We can do it your way"
'Cause he likes to think he's the boss!

P is for Papillon

Small in stature, big at heart

Tall fringed ears; a cutie

Call her "Butterfly," or Papillion

And fall in love with beauty

Right foot, left foot, see her frolic

Light foot, light heart prancing

Soft foot, sweet face, pocket-sized

Quite a showgirl dancing!

P is for Pug

Do you need a little friend

Who thinks that she's a noble?

A Pug is like the perfect blend

Of indolent and mobile!

She'll spin in circles, then run off

To hide behind a curtain

A fancy dog bed she may scoff

And sleep in yours for certain!

Some days she may even consent

To be a model pup

And play the part to the extent

That you can dress her up!

Q is for Qimmiq

Qimmiq is the name of the true Inuit dog

North America's rare and oldest breed

They could pull your sled to do an Arctic travelogue

Or take you to skijor at lightning speed

They have lived in Canada four thousand years or more

And nearly went extinct some years ago

But they were bravely saved by people who adore

This loyal gentle breed from head to toe

The Qimmiq lives in Nunavut, with Northern Lights above

They love the cold, that is no mystery

It is a perfect place for this living emblem of

A noble purebred Arctic history

Q is for Queensland Heeler

Queensland Heeler is a name for

The Australian Cattle Dog, or

Sometimes they're even called Red or Blue Heelers

They have a problem-solving knack

And it is a well-known fact,

That Heelers love to ride in your four-wheelers!

Give that dog something fun to do

Or else he may start herding you!

For Heelers are intended to move livestock

He's athletic and protective

Though rarely introspective

And would rather have a run than take a walk!

R is for Rhodesian Ridgeback

The "African Lion Dog"
Thinks his family's his pack
He'll protect them whatever occurs
This sleek shining dog
Has a ridge down his back,
That looks like a sword made of fur

The Rhodesian Ridgeback
Was bred to be brave
In what is now known as Zimbabwe,
But to be with his family's
The thing he most craves,
On the couch at the end of the day!

R is for Rottweiler

Intelligence defines this gentleman

The "Butcher's Dog" is always in control

Protecting, always watching for his clan

To be in charge is usually his goal

He likes to run around and have some fun,

And though he likes to think that he's the king

When all his guarding work is finally done

He can be quite the clowning, silly thing

Rottweilers are robust and confident

To work and family they are dutiful

You'll know him when you see this handsome gent

His black and russet coat is beautiful!

S is for Schipperke

That little black dog! See her on the boat,

With a ruff of long fur 'round her throat?

She never gets seasick, needs no antidote,

Just enjoys the salt spray on her coat

Agile and stubborn and smart as a whip

At strangers she'll bark and she'll yip,

She'll keep all the vermin from boarding your ship

And she'll be your companion round-trip!

S is for Skye Terrier

The Isle of Skye by Scotland lies

And is the home of merry Skyes

The Terriers tough and agile

And not remotely fragile

Their strength belies their size

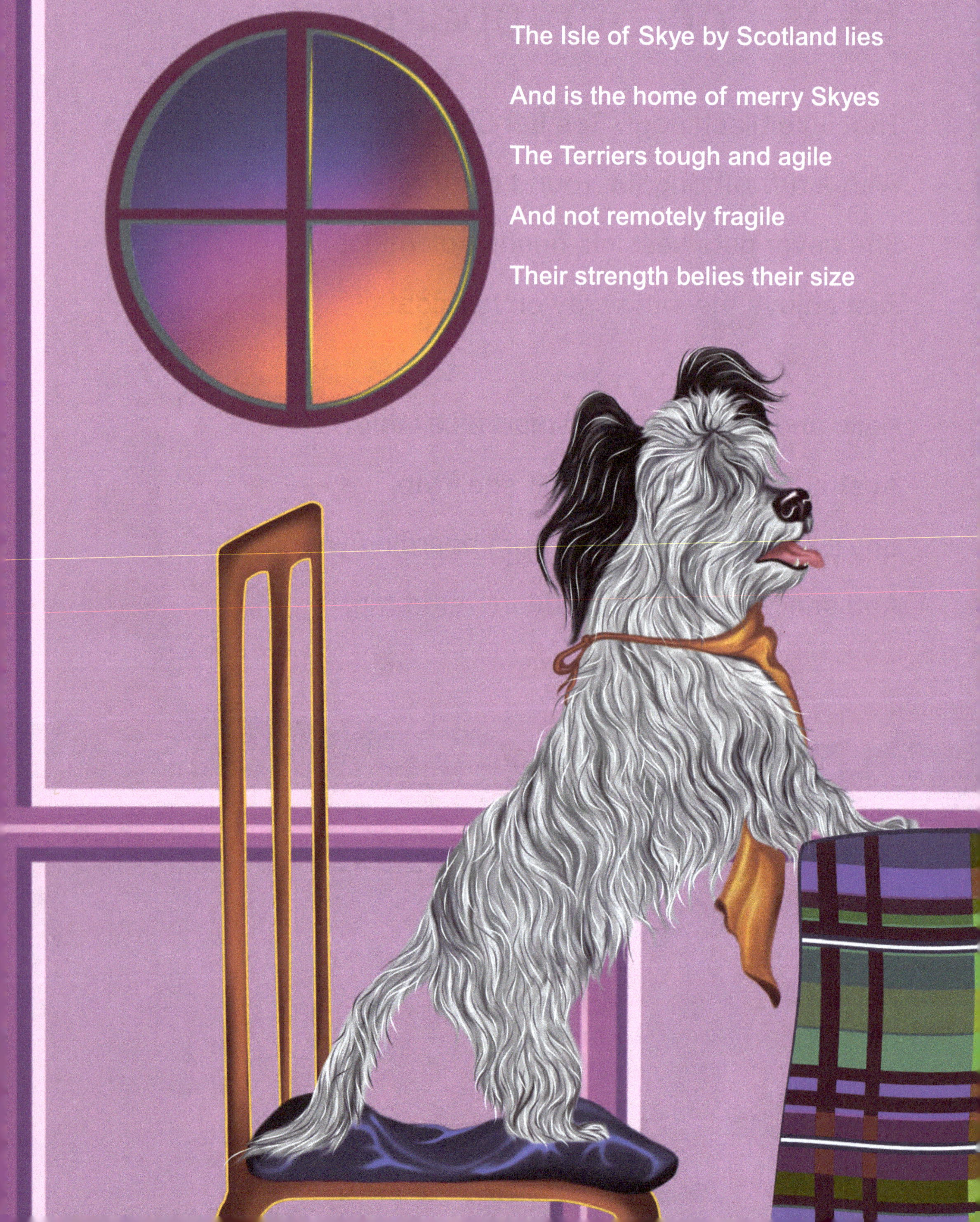

Though short in leg, they're long of back

And often use their nose to track

To find a fox or badger

You simply need to add your

Skye Terrier to the pack

Don't forget his coat needs grooming

When you train don't be presuming

He'll follow your command

Or do what you demand

For he may leave you fuming!

T is for Tibetan Mastiff
(A Haiku)

Night at the temple

Mastiff guardians walk free

Wise Tibetan eyes

Cat foot silent step

Keep the monastery safe

Swift and powerful

Nepal mountain dog

Peace and combat embodied

Equilibrium

T is for Treeing Walker Coonhound

Now doesn't that name make you want to smile?
A dog that can chase things up trees
She's able to track things for miles and miles
Then bay her success to the breeze
And cleans up with the greatest of ease!

The Walker's a worker, once she's on the job
And needs to be able to run
She's good with a family but may sometimes rob
A toy or a gadget for fun
Then hide it away when she's done

If you like a dog that will search through the forest
And maybe scale tall fences, too
Who can vocalize loudly, then might I suggest
The Walker's the talker for you
A true hunter's dog through and through!

U is for Umbwa Wa Ki-Shenzi

Umbwa Wa Ki-Shenzi is a unique name to say
That's "traditional dog" in Swahili
They're slender and they're speedy and they're quick to obey
And would rather always ramble freely

This South African hound is a truehearted sidekick
His lineage is mixed and goes way back
If you want a hunting dog, you just may want to pick
This member of the Africanis pack

U is for Utonagan
(You-teh-NAH-gun)

Here is a dog that looks just like a wolf
Although he has no wolf in him
He loves attention and his family
He's agile and active and trim

You can feel the true "Spirit of the Wolf"
When you see his golden-brown eyes
He'll jump with joy if he knows you or not
But howl when you say your goodbyes

Utonagans are very quick learners
They are quite a pleasure to own
They're eager to please, but easily bored
So don't leave them too long alone!

V is for Vizsla
(VEEZ-lah)

Is he a hungry dog, or a dog that is Hungarian?
Which do you suppose he ought to be?
He's such a classy canine, and not a rough barbarian
Sort of golden-red and running free!
You can take him out a-hunting, or a-walking in the park
He's smart and very trainable you see
So affectionate and active,
He's really quite attractive
And that's the way a Vizsla oughta be!

V is for Volpino Italiano

Do you suppose that Michelangelo
Had a dog in his painting studio?
Or maybe took it with him to and fro
While he painted his frescoed tableau?

Try to imagine his dog long ago
Watching him making the ceiling scenes glow,
A cute Volpino Italiano
Keeping watch from the floor down below

I'm sure that a dog would be apropos
For such a Renaissance artist to show
First peeks of the Sistine Chapel, although
He'd have to be careful and even so
The paints he used up there might overflow
Causing the poor doggy to undergo
Clean up of a spilled paint halo!

W is for Weimaraner

The Grey Ghost of Germany is famous for her beauty

Her stately grace, and angel's face

Might make you think she's snooty

But Weimaraners often get quite silly when they play

A pose they'll strike, for photos like

William Wegman's pup, "Man Ray"

Weimies love to romp and cuddle, chew toys or chase a bone

But they might scowl and even howl

If you leave them home alone!

W is for West Highland White Terrier

Westies, Westies, they're your besties!

Bonny Scots in red wool vesties!

They're pert, alert, and rarely curt,

Westies love to dig in the dirt!

These small white doggies travel well,

And as a guard dog, they are swell

When one latches his eye on you,

You'll see his piercing look shine through

With thick eyebrows and fuzzy snout

He'll win your heart, without a doubt!

X is for Xingopadoodle
(ZING-go-pah-DUDE-uhl)

What kind of dog would an alien own
If the alien came from Pluto?
Not a terrier or sighthound or herding-dog clone
Or a Nottingham-Skiddley Rizzuto!

No, there's only one dog Plutonians choose
They fall for it kit and caboodle,
And that is the one and only pup who's
The fabulous Xingopadoodle!

It's not like they have a big choice, don'tcha see,
For there really are no other breeds,
That live on their planet, and so it's decreed
Xingos meet all their pet owning needs

Their ears are quite curly
Their tails are all swirly
And their teeth are amazingly pearly
They wake very early
Their lashes are whirly
And their bark is a bit hurly-burly!

When they go for a walk, they sniff all the blocks
Of ice that make up the landscape
And they can be taught not to wipe snot
On your sleeve when you ask for a handshake

But the best thing of all, about this canine gem
Is they grow to unusual size
So big you can ride 'em, though it's quite hard to hide 'em
Or find them a decent disguise

It may be that someday we'll take our vacations
On really long trips throughout space,
And then we could meet the Plutonian Nations
And see their cool dogs face-to-face

Until then we'll have to imagine how they
Handle the ice and the cold while they play
We really don't know how they get through the day
With so little sunlight, the days must be gray
And we have to take care that we don't go astray
For Pluto is really quite far, far away!

X is for Xoloitzcuintli
(SHOW-low-eats-QUEENT-lee)

There is a dog called the Xoloitzcuintli,
I swear I did not make this up
He's also known as the "Mexican Hairless"
For he is a sleek, shiny pup

He's smooth as a cue ball, quite graceful and strong
Was sacred to Aztecs of yore
He's native to Mexico, been there a while
Maybe three thousand years or more!

He's not that well known, but well worth the knowing
And now that you know, say "hello,"
To a warm ball of fun (keep him out of the sun!)
I know you'll go wild for the Xolo!

Y is for Yarmouth Toller

Yarmouth Tollers are a canine delight

They're patient and smart and rarely uptight

They know how to attract

Ducks and geese with their act

In their fur of copper and white

If you've got a duck hunting fever

Try this dog and you'll be a believer

In the talents and grace of

And spirited pace of

Nova Scotia Duck Tolling Retrievers!

Y is for Yorkshire Terrier

A Yorkshire Terrier was found by a soldier
In a foxhole in World War II
They named her Smoky and took her along
And made her a part of the crew

Through tropical heat and C-ration food,
Through combat, and air raids, and storms
She flew with the crew on their recon missions
And learned a few tricks to perform

One day an airfield needed to run
A wire through a pipe underground
Brave Smoky forged through it, all 70 feet
While a string on her collar unwound

So if you've a need, for a friend who is brave
And smarts and small size come in handy,
You'd hardly do better than this little dog
The Yorkshire Terrier is dandy!

Z is for Zapadno-Sibirska Lajka
(ZAHP-ud-no see-BEER-ska LIE-kah)

Here are some nifty Russian words

That you will need to know

To talk about the dog that's loved

From Krasnoyarsk* to Moscow

Zapadno is the first word,

It's "west" to you and me

Sibirska means "Siberian"

That's where he's from you see

* KRASS-nigh-arsk

And now we come to Lajka

Which is very apt, you know

For it means "barker," which he is

When hunting he does go

His fur is thick and deep and warm

With tail curved over back

He'd love to hike the trails with you

If you like to backpack

He's bred for hunting and is quite brave

At treeing bears at dawn

But do not ask him to stay home

Alone while you are gone

For being penned with naught to do

Never really suffices,

He's much too clever to be left

To his own devices!

Keep him busy doing things

Whatever else you do,

He's canny, and soon you may find

This Russian dog trains you!

Z is for Zuchon
(ZOO-kaan)

Who is this tiny puppy
Looking like a teddy bear?
With his wide-set shiny eyes
And his soft and curly hair?

He's a cross between a Shih Tzu
And a sweet Bichon Frisé,
And he'll sure be pleased to meet you
'Cause he really loves to play

Whether you call him a Zuchon
Or a Teddy Bear or Shichon,
This hybrid dog may catch on
So you'd better keep a leash on
Your pet so he can't stray,
Don't let him lose his way
Or sashay far away,
And end up in San Tropez!
Okay?

And Don't Forget Cats!

Quirky and cryptic and often quite funny
Sometimes aloof, at other times chummy
A cat may well sprawl
And then try to maul
Your hand if you tickle her tummy

Most every tabby knows his ancestors slept
On lap rugs and cushions in ancient Egypt
He won't be denied
His tribute or pride
And expects to be very well kept

Kitties are wonderful as pets and as friends
Their snuggles and hijinks are great dividends
Cats seem to judge us
Then gently nudge us
To see things through a feline lens

Gingers, tuxedos, black, white, or calico
Siamese, Manx, Maine Coon, or Bambino
Your furry familiar
Will frolic and then purr
All hail to the Glorious Gato!

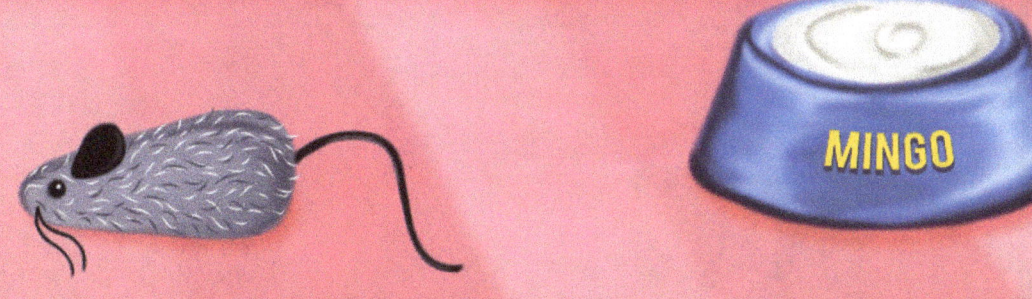

Finale

So now that you have read about

All of these canines

You may be thinking "I want one!

A dog that is all mine!"

And I think that you would do well

To get a four-legged friend

Be it purebred or a crossbreed

Or a fifty-something blend!

Go down to your local shelter

Or breed rescue place

And look real close, right in the eyes

Of every furry face

You might be tempted to just look
At puppies, 'cause they're cute
But don't pass by the grown-up dogs
Or those with graying snoots

All dogs need love and happy homes
And humans who are kind
Even dogs that have three legs
And hounds that are half blind

Just be sure you have the time
To feed and train and groom
Your newfound friend, and that you have
The space to give them room

The love and care that you give to
A rescued dog will be
Returned to you a hundred times
Each day unfailingly!

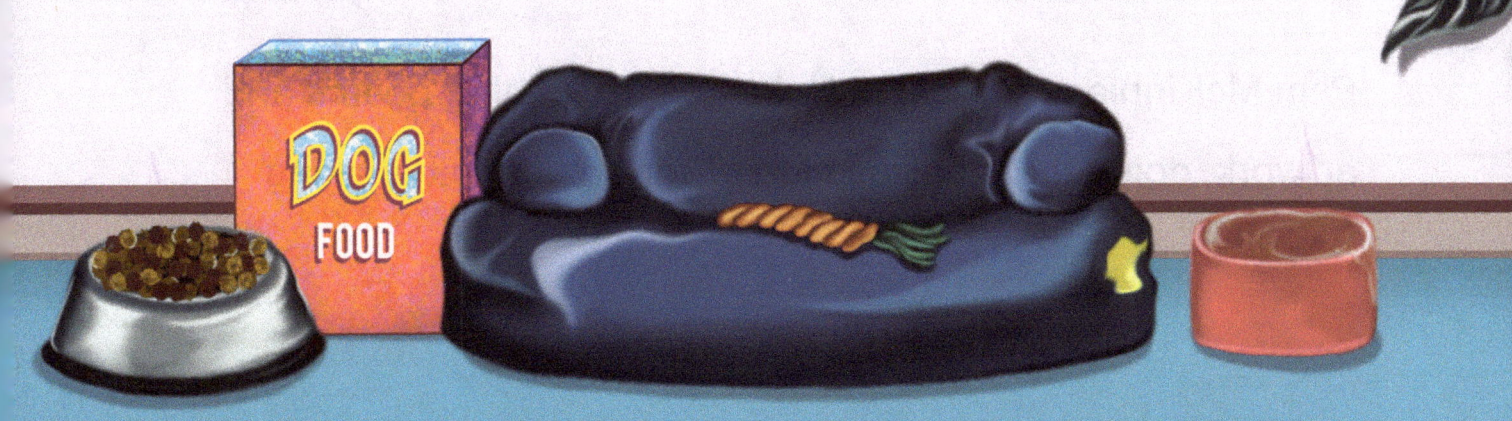

Acknowledgements

Thank you to everyone who has ever read parts of The Arfabet, or sat and listened to me read it, or said to keep going on it. Poetry isn't an easy thing to share with others, so thank you for the encouragement.

Special thanks to:

Bruce, for not letting me off the hook on getting published, for reading the really early drafts, and encouraging the process.

Almir Ulises Mestre León and Aram Joao Mestre León for months of work on the beautiful illustrations which are based off of some very short descriptions and which are filled with their wonderful ideas, talent, and the vivid colors that give the poems life. Also, huge thanks to Matthew Pippin for connecting me with these wonderful artists.

Pam McKinnie at Concepts Unlimited, for joining poems and artwork, doing the thankless job of formatting and making things fit, making suggestions, assuring me that this book could indeed come to life, and knowing all those bits of publishing arcana that support and improve a book.

Nicole Villacres and Christina Hill, my ride-or-die BFFs, who let me read some of these poems on the *Greetings From Nowhere* podcast.

The attendees of the "Four Minutes of Fame" events put on by Write On The River who listened to some of the poems and politely applauded.

Larry Queen, who has listened to me
  Yap, howl
    Whine, growl
      Whimper and yowl
        About writing and editing.

About the Author

Photo by Persephone Sapphora

TJ Farrell grew up in Colorado and lives in Wenatchee, Washington. She makes up silly little rhymes at the drop of a hat and inappropriately inserts them into conversations. This book was a labor of love inspired by everyone who ever showed her a picture of their pet, and the amazing diversity of the canine world. She also acts in local theater, makes over-the-top Halloween costumes, does voice acting, podcasts with her friends, and enjoys playing Dungeons and Dragons and video games.

About the Illustrators

Aram Joao Mestre León (@aramjoao92) and Almir Ulises Mestre León (@almir_lion_drawings) are twin self-taught illustrators based in Las Tunas, Cuba. Since a young age they've been drawn to the world of storytelling and self-expression through colorful images, usually their artworks contain elements of fantasy.

Illustrators Continued

Aram's Illustrations: *Introductory Poem, Afghan Hound, Alaskan Malamute, Border Collie, Collie, Dachshund, English Cocker Spaniel, English Setter, Finnish Spitz, Irish Wolfhound, Italian Greyhound, Jindo, Labrador Retriever, Löwchen, Mutt, Newfoundland, Norwich Terrier, Otterhound, Papillon, Queensland Heeler, Rottweiler, Tibetan Mastiff, Treeing Walker Coonhound, Umbwa Wa Ki-Shenzi, Weimaraner, Xoloitzcuintli, Yarmouth Toller, Zapadno-Sibirska Lajka, Zuchon.*

Almir's Illustrations: *Cover, Title Page, Basenji, Chinese Crested, Dalmatian, French Bulldog, German Shepherd, Great Dane, Harrier, Havanese, Japanese Chin, Keeshond, Kuvasz, Mastiff, Old English Sheepdog, Pug, Qimmiq, Rhodesian Ridgeback, Schipperke, Skye Terrier, Utonagan, Vizsla, Volpino Italiano, West Highland White Terrier, Xingopadoodle, Yorkshire Terrier, Cat, Finale Poem.*

www.ingramcontent.com/pod-product-compliance
Lightning Source LLC
Chambersburg PA
CBHW080559090426
42735CB00016B/3285